Published in 2013 by The Rosen Publishing Group, Inc.
29 East 21st Street, New York, NY 10010

Photo Credits: **KEY** tl=top left; tc=top center; tr=top right; cl=center left; c=center; cr=center right; bl=bottom left; bc=bottom center; br=bottom right; bg=background
CBT = Corbis; CCD = Corel Corp; iS = istockphoto.com; SH = Shutterstock; TF = Topfoto

front cover br, cl CBT; cr CCD; bg iS; **2–3**bg iS; **4–5**bg iS; **7**tr iS; **8–9**bg iS; **9**br iS; **10**tr iS; **10–11**bg iS; **11**bg iS; **12**bl CCD; bl iS; **12–13**c CBT; **13**br, cr CBT; **14**tr CBT; bl iS; br SH; bl TF; **14–15**bg iS; bg CCD; **16–17**bg iS; **17**br iS; **18**tl TF; **18–19**bg CBT; **19**tr iS; **20**c CBT; **20–21**bg iS; **21**cr CBT; tl CCD; **22**bc CBT; bg iS; **22–23**tc CBT; **23**cr CBT; bg, tr iS; **24**bl CBT; bl iS; tr SH; **24–25**bg CBT; bg iS; **25**bc, bg, tl CBT; bc, cl, cr iS; cr SH; **26**tl iS; **26–27**bg iS; **27**tl iS; **28**br, br iS; tl TF; **28–29**bg iS; **30**cr CCD; **31**bg iS; **32**bg iS

All illustrations copyright Weldon Owen Pty Ltd

Weldon Owen Pty Ltd
Managing Director: Kay Scarlett
Creative Director: Sue Burk
Publisher: Helen Bateman
Senior Vice President, International Sales: Stuart Laurence
Vice President Sales North America: Ellen Towell
Administration Manager, International Sales: Kristine Ravn

Library of Congress Cataloging-in-Publication Data

Costain, Meredith.
 Native Americans of the great plains / by Meredith Costain.
    p. cm. — (Discovery education: Ancient civilizations)
 Includes index.
 ISBN 978-1-4777-0052-5 (library binding) — ISBN 978-1-4777-0089-1 (pbk.) —
 ISBN 978-1-4777-0090-7 (6-pack)
 1. Indians of North America—Great Plains—History—Juvenile literature. 2. Indians of North America—Great Plains—Social life and customs—Juvenile literature. I. Title.
 E78.G73C66 2013
 978.004'97—dc23
                    2012019580

CPSIA Compliance Information: Batch #W13PK2: For Further Information contact Rosen Publishing, New York, New York at 1-800-237-9932

Discovery
EDUCATION™

ANCIENT CIVILIZATIONS

NATIVE AMERICANS OF THE GREAT PLAINS

MEREDITH COSTAIN

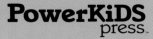
PowerKiDS
press™

New York

Contents

Home on the Great Plains

More than 30 different tribes of Native Americans lived in the Great Plains area of North America. This vast area ranged from the chilly foothills of the Rocky Mountains in the northwest, to the much warmer Mississippi Valley in the south. Tribes such as the Cheyenne, the Blackfoot, and the Sioux grew corn, hunted wild animals, and lived in cone-shaped structures made from poles and buffalo hide, called tepees.

Family home
A tepee was set up so its steeper, rear side was against westerly winds. The doorway faced east, toward the rising Sun. Families kept all of their possessions inside their tepee, which formed a single large living space.

A land of contrasts
Tribes of Native Americans spread across the continent, from the freezing waters of the Arctic coast to the warmer southeast. The Great Plains area is in the center of this map.

SUBARCTIC

ARCTIC

NORTH WEST COAST

PLATEAU

CALIFORNIA

GREAT BASIN

GREAT PLAINS

NORTHEAST

SOUTHWEST

SOUTHEAST

Smoke flaps
Two long poles were used to open the smoke flaps to make a smoke hole.

TEPEE CAMP

A large group would set up their camp of tepees in a circle. There were strict rules of behavior inside tepees. An open door was a sign that visitors were welcome. Men entered to the right, women to the left. No one walked between the fire and someone else. When the host cleaned his pipe, it was time for visitors to leave.

C-shaped camp
A tepee camp was set up so it formed a C shape, with the opening facing east.

Entrance
The oval or V-shaped entrance to the tepee had a door flap made of animal skin, which was easy to pull open.

Cooking fire
The fire was set up beneath the smoke hole for the smoke to escape. The woodpile was near the door.

On the Move

Tepees could be easily folded and carried when their owners needed to move to a new place to find food or to escape from enemies. At first, dogs were used to pull loads on a travois—two poles with a platform made of animal hide stretched between them. Later, horses (brought to North America by Spanish explorers) were used to pull the travois instead. Toboggans, snowshoes, and dogsleds helped people to travel across snow in winter.

Spirit dogs

The people of the Great Plains called their much-loved horses spirit dogs or medicine dogs. As well as being a status symbol, horses allowed them to move around easily to hunt buffalo and antelope or to fight battles. The men, who had a special bond with their horse, usually rode bareback. The women used saddles, which were often highly decorated.

Water transportation

Boats were used for fishing, carrying goods, and moving between hunting grounds. The Chumash of California built canoes from planks of pine. Other tribes built their canoes from birch bark or dugout cedar logs. Mandan women rowed bullboats (below) made from buffalo hides and willow.

SIGN LANGUAGE

As the people of North America separated into different groups, the way they spoke slowly changed and new languages developed. Tribes invented sign language so they could communicate with their neighbors. Instead of using words to make peace bargains or discuss trade, they used their hands.

Hello

Riding a horse

Peace

Friend

Buffalo Hunt

Buffalo were very important to the Plains tribes. In addition to their meat being a source of food, every part of the animal had a use—nothing was wasted. Their hairy hides were used to make clothing and tepee covers. Bones were used to make tools and sled runners. Eating utensils and gunpowder holders were made from horns, cooking pots from stomachs, campfire fuel from dung, and candles and soap from body fat.

BUFFALO JUMP

For thousands of years, hunters on the Great Plains guided buffalo herds to a cliff, then created a stampede, forcing the buffalo over the edge. Head-Smashed-In, in the Porcupine Hills of southern Alberta, in Canada, is a famous buffalo jump.

Buffalo herded over a cliff

Hunting methods

Hunters used several different ways to hunt and kill buffalo. Some buffalo were herded over cliffs or into deep snow. Others would be lured into a ravine by a hunter dressed in buffalo robes, then killed with spears. If the hunters were riding horses, they would chase the herd into a confined area, getting as close as they possibly could to an animal before shooting it with a bow and arrow or a gun.

Did You Know?

The Plains tribes had great respect for buffalo. They always thanked the spirits for a kill and regarded slain buffalo as having sacrificed their lives so the tribe could live.

Food and Meals

While the men were out hunting, the women stayed in the camp collecting, preparing, cooking, and storing food. There were no set mealtimes. People ate when they were hungry, after a good hunt, or when visitors arrived. Food was always shared out equally, even when there was not much to go around. Most tribes preserved and stored food for the winter months, when game animals and plants were harder to find.

SUN-DRIED FOOD

Food was collected in the warmer months when it was plentiful. Then it was preserved so it could be stored for use during winter. Buffalo meat was cut into thin strips and either hung from wooden frames or spread out on platforms to dry in the sun. Fish, wild berries, corn, and other vegetables were also preserved by being sun-dried.

...ts and pans

...als could be cooked outside using
...sic equipment. Corn bread was baked
...an outdoor oven. Meat was roasted
...er a fire or cooked in pits or containers
...ade from animal skins or buffalo
...omach. These were filled with water
...d hot stones, and this stewed the
...eat. European traders supplied metal
...oking pots and copper kettles, which
...ade cooking much easier.

Gathering food

Women spent hours every day looking for
food. Berries, plums, roots, and greens were
just some of the foods growing naturally.
Leftover berries were ground with dried
meat and fat to make a nutritious food
called pemmican, which kept for months.

Picking berries

There were more than 40 varieties of berry
growing in the wild, including blueberries
and raspberries.

Corn

Women and children cleaned and ground the
harvest of corn, then turned it into tortillas
and bread.

Clothing

Although Native Americans wore highly decorated clothing for ceremonies, their everyday outfits were more practical. Men wore loincloths or shirts or tunics with leggings. Women wore loose-fitting dresses or tunics, skirts, and leggings. People added cloaks and shawls in the winter months. Clothing was made from animal skins—deer, buffalo, moose, or rabbit—stitched together with bone needles and thread made from animal sinews.

Different styles
Each Native American tribe had its own distinctive style of clothing. This chief and his wife are from the Blackfoot tribe.

TANNING BUFFALO HIDE

Plains tribes made most of their clothing from tanned buffalo hide. First, women stretched the hide, then scraped it to remove the fat and flesh. They worked a mixture of cooked animal brains into the hide before drying it in the sun. The hide was then soaked and dried again. The final step was to soften the hide by pulling it back and forth over a tree branch.

Tanned and decorated buffalo hide

Beaded moccasins
Hand-stitched leather moccasins had hard or soft soles. They were decorated with dyed porcupine quills and elaborate beadwork.

Ceremonial clothing

Both men and women wore ceremonial robes on special occasions. These were made from soft buckskin, decorated with fringing and porcupine quills. Male chiefs and warriors from some Plains tribes wore full-length war bonnets, made from rows of eagle feathers and decorated with ermine tails and fancy beadwork.

War bonnet
A Plains tribe warrior wears his feathered war bonnet and carries his coup stick. Each feather in a war bonnet had to be earned by an act of bravery.

Growing Up

Babies were carried around on their mother's back, strapped snugly into a cradleboard. As they grew older, children were looked after by a large family of parents, aunts, uncles, and grandparents. Instead of going to school, they learned new skills by copying adults. By the time they were 13 years old, they knew all they needed to become an active member of the tribe.

Storytelling

A tribe's history and heritage were passed down from generation to generation through storytelling. Some stories told of the heroic deeds of the tribe's ancestors.

Young and old
Families gathered around a tribal elder for storytelling sessions. Legends and fables explained how local animals and plants came to be.

Ball games

Many tribes played ball games such as lacrosse or stickball. Lacrosse, sometimes called "little brother of war," was fast, violent, and could go on all day. Sports and games helped men and boys to develop hunting and fighting skills and to test their strength, courage, and staying power.

Goalposts

Deerskin ball

Netted racket

A baby's name was often chosen by relatives or elders rather than the child's parents.

LEARNING NEW SKILLS

Children were educated in tribal ways by their elders. Boys learned how to make tools and weapons, and how to hunt and fight. Girls were taught domestic skills, such as food preparation, pottery, basket-weaving, sewing, beadwork, and embroidery. Both the boys and girls were taught the tribe's traditional dances.

Target practice
Sioux boys were taught how to use bows and arrows, with jackrabbits as their target.

POWWOWS

A powwow is a gathering where Native Americans celebrate the circle of life with seasonal ceremonies of feasting, singing, and drumming. Originally, dances were performed for religious ceremonies, before warriors went hunting or into battle, or after they returned. Now, Native American from many tribes come together to celebrate and reaffirm their heritage and traditions.

The tradition continues
Powwows are joyous celebrations that honor Native American life and tradition. Held all over North America, they feature singing, dancing, and crafts, and often involve the local community. Traditional dancers perform at many powwows through the summer.

The drum is the heartbeat of a powwow. It connects drummers, singers, and dancers.

PIPE CEREMONY

Native Americans held solemn pipe-smoking rituals at powwows to ask for the spirits' help to make war or a peace treaty, or to bring rain. They might also ask for a hunt to be successful or for a good trade pact or bargain to be sealed.

Smoking pipe
The bowl of a smoking pipe was made from clay, wood, or soft soapstone. The stem was hollow wood.

The circle of life

To celebrate the circle of life, a powwow is often set up in a series of large circles. In the center is the dance arena, known as the arbor. Drummers and dancers form the next circle, and are surrounded by spectators and booths.

Spiritual Life

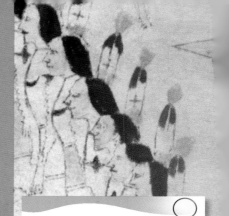

Plains tribes took care to live in harmony with the natural world, respecting the land and animals around them. They worshipped the Great Spirit, who had created them and all living things. They believed that the sky, Earth, plants, and animals—even the rivers and mountains—had spirits that must be respected. These spirits could be reached through dance, song, and prayer.

Did You Know?

To explain where thunderstorms came from, medicine men told stories about the Thunderbird, which had the power to produce thunder and lightning.

Sun dance
Many of the tribes performed different versions of the Sun dance, which was an offering to the Great Spirit in return for safety and prosperity. The dance went on for several days and only men took part. In some versions, dancers leaped or crawled in a large circle around a tall pole while gazing at the Sun.

Tribal elders

Members of a tribe respected the knowledge and wisdom of their elders. Tribes were led by a chief, who was chosen for his strength, bravery, and wisdom. Chiefs ruled with the help of warriors and other elders skilled in healing and spiritual knowledge.

Symbol of the circle

A Shoshone warrior wears traditional war dress. The circle painted around his horse's eye symbolizes the cycle of life and death. Native Americans believe the Great Spirit caused everything in the natural world—the Sun, the sky, the Moon, Earth—to be round.

Healers and Medicine

When people became sick, they were treated by healers called shamans, or medicine men and women. Shamans used herbs to treat illnesses and performed healing rituals with music and dancing. They spoke with the spirits and received help and guidance from them. They also asked the spirits to protect the tribe's warriors or to send rain.

Preparing medicine
While preparing medicine, a shaman chants and shakes a rattle to call for help from the spirits. Medicines were made from crushed leaves and powdered bark and roots.

Medicine dance
A group of people perform an elk medicine dance. Medicine dances were performed to ask the spirits for help with healing or perhaps to end a drought.

FAMOUS SHAMAN AND CHIEF

The Sioux chief Tatanka Iyotake, known as Sitting Bull, is one of the best known Native American leaders. While he was revered for his fearlessness in battle, he was also generous and wise. Sitting Bull became a shaman in his early twenties and believed strongly in visions.

Leader
Chief Sitting Bull (1831–1890) was made leader of the united Sioux tribes in 1867.

Medicine kit
Shamans kept their medicines in kits like this rawhide bag. Kits also held beads, bones, and stones believed to have special powers, which were wrapped in skins or cloth.

Arts and Crafts

Native Americans made beautiful objects for everyday use. Their arts and crafts, with bold colors, patterns, and designs, are now famous all over the world. Ceremonial clothing and sacred objects such as bowls, rattles, and pipes were richly decorated. The objects had special meanings for their owners, either as a record of their life and achievements or as a way of showing their position in the tribe. Some designs told stories or were linked with the spirits.

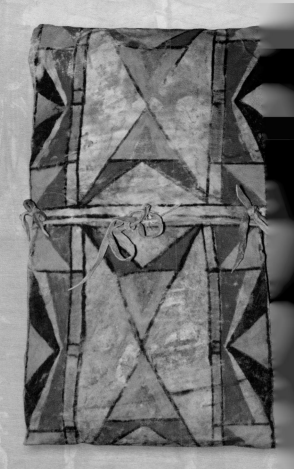

WEAVING

People from the Navajo tribe wove cloth with bold and colorful patterns from cotton and wool. They also made blankets that were warm, soft, and light. These chief's blankets (below) were given as gifts to leaders of other tribes. The Navajo planted and grew the cotton themselves and kept flocks of sheep that had originally come from Spanish colonists.

Patterns and designs
This decorated parfleche is made from buffalo hide. Parfleches were large containers used for storing dried meat on long journeys. The patterns often symbolized long life or the seasons.

Did You Know?
The Zuni believed that the spirits of plants and animals lived inside objects that looked like them. Called fetishes, they were either naturally shaped stones or carved objects.

Breastplate
This breastplate has been decorated with porcupine quills, colored beads, and fringing made from animal hide.

Beadwork

Beads were mostly used to decorate clothing and moccasins. At first, Native Americans made beads from natural materials—shells, animal bones, horns, teeth, stones, and amber. After European traders arrived, they used glass beads as well. The color combinations, styles, and stitches varied from tribe to tribe. Plains beadwork featured the intricate peyote stitch. The Northern tribes used floral patterns in their designs. Eastern Woodlands tribes made ceremonial belts from white and purple shells.

Tomahawk
A beaded tassel hangs from the intricately carved wooden handle of a tomahawk. The blade was made of stone and, later, metal.

Moccasins
Moccasins were sewn from buffalo hide and deerskin. They were often decorated with intricate beadwork.

Warfare

The different tribes often quarreled over the best hunting or farming grounds. Sometimes, they went to war to avenge their people or to gain battle honors. Although they sometimes tortured or scalped prisoners, warriors were more likely to carry out night hit-and-run raids on enemy camps to steal their horses. Plains warriors fought with bows and arrows, knives, tomahawks, clubs, and spears.

Warrior chief
A brave who had fought well was entitled to become a warrior chief and dress in ceremonial clothing.

Signs of bravery

It was possible to tell what kind of warrior a man was by the type of feather he wore. These were known as coup feathers, because an act of bravery such as striking down or scalping an enemy or stealing their horses was known as a coup.

Throat cut
If the top of the feather was clipped diagonally, the wearer had cut his enemy's throat.

Scalped
If a notch was cut into the feather, the wearer had both cut his enemy's throat and scalped him.

Multiple wounds
Split feathers showed that the wearer had been wounded many times in battle.

WARHORSES

The warriors of the Great Plains depended on their warhorses on the battlefield. The horses shared any battle honors that their owner won, and were painted with the same symbols of achievement or loss as those marked on their owner's body.

Battledress
A warhorse's tail was often trimmed, dyed, and decorated with eagle feathers.

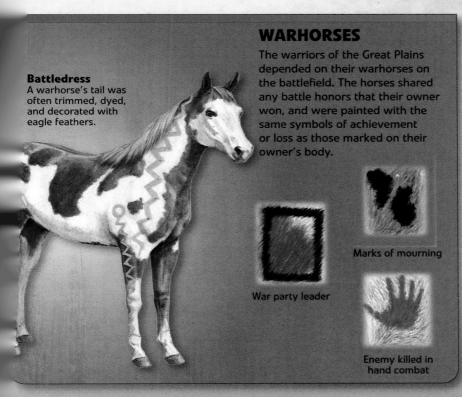

War party leader

Marks of mourning

Enemy killed in hand combat

War trophy
Some tribes removed the scalps of their enemies, believing that this brought them honor. A scalp was thought to contain the dead person's soul.

Multiple coups
Feathers that had many jagged edges announced that the wearer had struck down many enemies.

Single wound
If the feather was dyed red, this indicated that the wearer had been wounded in battle.

Enemy killed
A red spot on a feather was a sign that the wearer had killed his enemy.

Massacre at Wounded Knee Creek
In 1890, many members of the Sioux tribe lost their lives
while resisting efforts by the US cavalry to move them
from their homeland in present-day South Dakota.

Changing Times

During the nineteenth century, European colonists began taking over Native American tribal homelands for farming. In 1830, a law was passed that allowed the government to set up reservations for Native Americans who had been forced off their land. Although reservation schools taught the ways of white people, Native Americans never forgot where they had come from and their connection to the land, and passed on their customs and traditions to their children.

ARRIVAL OF THE RAILROAD

In the 1860s, work began on a railroad that would run across the continent of North America, linking the east and west coasts. The buffalo herds that roamed the Great Plains were slaughtered to make way for the railroad tracks. This reduced the Native American population, who, without buffalo, faced starvation.

That's Amazing!

Between 1872 and 1874, more than 3.5 million buffalo were slaughtered by European settlers to make way for cattle and farms. By 1900, fewer than 1,000 buffalo were left.

The Trail of Tears

About 15,000 Cherokee, along with members of other tribes, were forced by soldiers to leave their land and march west to a reservation. The route is known as the Trail of Tears. Many suffered exposure, starvation, and disease along the way. By the journey's end, 4,000 people had died.

Make Your Own Tepee

Native Americans made tepees with branches and buffalo hide. Make your own model using paper and sticks. Decorate it with some of the designs found in this book.

What you need:

- ☑ 4 sticks or twigs, about 1 foot (30 cm) long
- ☑ A rubber band or piece of twine
- ☑ A piece of scrap paper
- ☑ A pencil
- ☑ Scissors
- ☑ A large paper grocery bag or 11 x 17 inch (28 x 43 mm) sheet of heavy paper
- ☑ Markers, colored pencils, crayons, or paints
- ☑ Tape

1 Gather the sticks together. Loosely bind them with the rubber band or twine about 2.5 inches (6.35 cm) from the top. Spread the sticks out to form a triangle.

2 Holding the tepee frame flat over the scrap paper, use a pencil to trace the outline of one side of the tepee. Cut out the triangular shape.

3 Open out the grocery bag or use a large sheet of heavy paper. Place the triangle shape on the paper and trace around its outline.

4 Place the shape down next to the first triangle with the long edges touching. Trace around it. Do this twice more.

5 Cut out the new shape around the outside edge. Cut out a small door from one of the triangles.

6 Decorate the "outside" of the paper with symbols and patterns.

7 Fold the "inside" of the paper along each of the pencil lines to get a sharp crease. Place a stick along each fold, to form an internal frame. Tape the sticks into place.

8 Form the paper into a tepee shape. Snip off the top to allow the sticks to poke through. Tape the edges together.

Enjoy your tepee!

Glossary

cher (AHR-cher) A person
o shoots with a bow
d arrow.

venge (uh-VENJ) To take
venge on behalf of someone.

uffalo jump
UH-fuh-loh JUMP) A cliff
here buffalo were guided to
mp over the edge by Native
merican hunters.

olonists (KAH-luh-nists)
eople who settle in a
ew country.

radleboard (KRAY-dul-bord)
wooden frame, worn on the
ack, used by Native American
women for carrying an infant.

Great Plains (GRAYT PLAYNZ)
A vast grassland region of central
North America extending from
the Canadian provinces of
Alberta, Saskatchewan, and
Manitoba southward to Texas.

Great Spirit (GRAYT SPIR-ut)
The chief god of many Native
American tribes.

lacrosse (luh-KROS) A ball
game invented by Native
Americans, now played by two
teams using long-handled,
hooked sticks fitted with netted
pouches to propel a ball into
each other's goal.

massacre (MA-sih-ker) To kill
large numbers of people or
animals indiscriminately.

pemmican (PEH-mih-kuhn)
Food prepared by Native
Americans from lean, dried strips
of meat pounded into paste,
mixed with fat and berries, and
pressed into small cakes.

powwow (POW-wow)
A ceremony held by Native
Americans, usually accompanied
by feasting and dancing, for
requests such as the cure of a
disease or success in a hunt.

preserve (prih-ZURV) To treat
food to stop it from decaying.

quills (KWILZ)
Sharp, hollow spines of a
porcupine or hedgehog.

ravine (ruh-VEEN) A deep,
narrow valley or river gorge.

reservation
(reh-zer-VAY-shun) An area of
public land set aside for a special
purpose, for example, a Native
American tribe that has been
removed from its original
hunting ground.

shaman (SHAY-min) A
medicine man or woman who
has the ability to speak with
the spirits.

sign language
(SYN LANG-gwij) Physical
gestures for communication
between two speakers of
different languages.

sinews (SIN-yooz)
Cords of muscle that connect
tissue to bone.

travois (truh-VOY)
A transportation vehicle made
from two poles, with a platform
made of animal hide stretched
between them, which is pulled
by an animal.

Index

Websites

Due to the changing nature of Internet links, PowerKids Press has developed an online list of websites related to the subject of this book. This site is updated regularly. Please use this link to access the list:
www.powerkidslinks.com/disc/native/